I0769958

The Story of a Special Day
Volume 319

November 14

*The 318th day of the year (319th in leap years).
There are 47 days remaining until the end of the year.*

by Michael Dobson

Timespinner
Press

Watch for e-book editions for Kindle, e-pub devices, and other formats from your favorite online booksellers.

For more information about the series, about us, or about your special day, please email us at editor@timespinnerpress.com.

Look for other volumes in *The Story of a Special Day*, coming often. See www.timespinnerpress.com for details and for the most recent information.

Table of Contents

For the definition of "O.S.," "CE," and "BCE" used with some dates , see the section "On Names and Dates."

Cover: "First Airplane Takeoff from a Warship," US Naval History and Heritaga Command. This event took place November 14, 1910 — the COVER STORY and EVENT OF THE DAY.

Quote of the Day

"What experience and history teach is this — that nations and governments have never learned anything from history, or acted upon any lessons they might have drawn from it."

Georg Wilhelm Friedrich Hegel, philosopher
died November 14, 1831

3

 Michael Dobson

Labors of the Months: November, by Simon Bening

November 14 in History

While some days of the year are more famous than others, every day of the year is filled with important, exciting, and unusual events, from religious awakenings to natural disasters, from wars to breakthroughs in technology, and from tragedy to triumph.

In this section, you'll learn about all the events that make November 14 important, including the special event that makes up our cover story or event of the day. Some events you may already know about, others may be new to you, but all of them are important parts of the history of the work.

Let's explore some of the reasons why November 14 is a very special day!

Eugene Ely and his Curtiss Pusher

What Happened on November 14?

From the creation of great works of engineering and art, to devastating wars and natural disasters, thousands of years of history have left their mark on each and every day. Here are some important events that occurred on November 14. (Ilustrated items are highlighted.)

Event of the Day/Cover Story
1910 - First Airplane Takes Off From a Ship

Exhibition pilot Eugene Ely took off from the light cruiser USS *Birmingham* in a Curtiss Model D Pusher on November 14, 1910. This was the first takeoff of an airplane from a ship.

The US Army's aviation program began June 28, 1909, with a demonstration of the Wright 1909 Military Flyer (now on display at the Smithsonian's National Air and Space Museum). Not to be outdone, the US Navy assigned Captain Washington Irving Chambers to investigate naval aviation potential.

Chambers contacted Glenn Curtiss, aviation pioneer who founded the Curtiss Aeroplane and Motor Company. Curtiss and Ely met with Chambers in October 1910 to plan two experimental flights.

For the first flight, a temporary platform 83 feet long was built on the bow of the USS *Birmingham*. The airplane lost altitude immediately on clearing the platform, and the wheels dipped into the water before Ely was able to get the plane back under control. His goggles were covered with spray, making it difficult to see, so Ely landed on a nearby beach rather than circle the harbor and land at the Norfolk (Virginia) Navy Yard as originally planned.

Two months later, on January 18, 1911, Ely reversed the feat in San Francisco and made the first successful shipboard landing of an aircraft.

Ely hoped to join the new Naval aviation program, but it wasn't yet organized enough. Chambers urged Ely to give up exhibition flying for the sake of safety, Ely replied, "I guess I will be like the rest of them, keep at it until I am killed."

On October 19, 1911, flying in Macon, Georgia, he died in a plane crash. He was posthumously awarded the Distinguised Flying Cross.

Eugene Ely approaches the deck of the USS *Pennsylvania*, January 18, 1911, the first landing of an airplane on a warship

1851 — Herman Melville's novel *Moby-Dick* is first published in the US. (It was published October 18, 1851, in the UK.) It was a commercial failure during the author's lifetime, but was rediscovered in the early 20th century and is now considered one of the great American novels.

1889 — Pioneering female reporter Elizabeth Seaman, better known by her pen name **Nellie Bly, begins her record-breaking trip around the world**. Originally inspired by Jules Verne's 1873 novel *Around the World in Eighty Days*, Nellie Bly achieved her goal in only 72 days.

Nellie Bly (Photo: H. J. Myers)

1940 — The **Coventry Blitz**, a series of bombing raids by the Luftwaffe during World War II's Battle of Britain, has its most devastating night when 515 bombers attack, damaging more than two-thirds of the city's buildings, including Coventry Cathedral.

Winston Churchill visits the ruins of Coventry Cathedral

1957 — A summit meeting of the **American Mafia** takes place in Apalachin, New York. Local police, noticing the suspiciously large number of expensive cars from around the country, raid the meeting, capturing over 60 underworld bosses and confirming the existence of the American Mafia to the public.

1960 — During the New Orleans school desegregation crisis, six-year old **Ruby Bridges** becomes the first African-American student to attend the William Frantz Elementary School. She required a US Marshal escort to attend safely, captured in a famous Norman Rockwell painting, "The Problem We All LIve With."

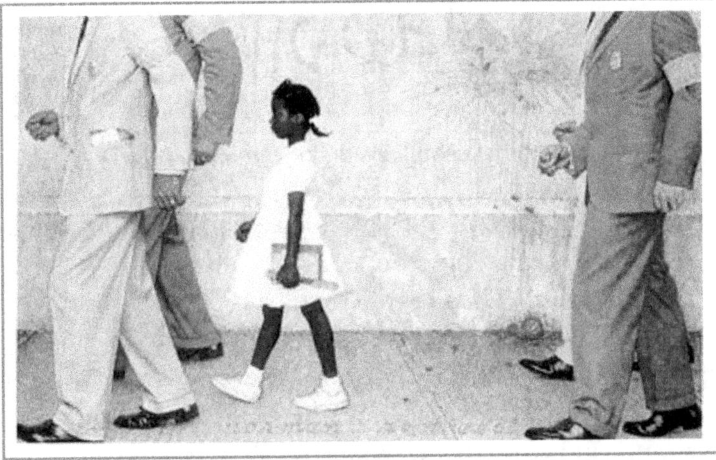

"The Problem We All Live With, " by Norman Rockwell. Six-year old Ruby Bridges is escorted to elementary school by US marshals.

1965 — Vietnam War: The **first major battle** between US Army forces and the North Vietnamese Army, the Battle of Ia Drang, begins. It will last until November 18, 1965. Both sides claimed victory. *(Photo next page.)*

US Army combat operations during the Battle of la Drang

1969 — **Apollo 12**, the second crewed mission to the Moon, takes off. The crew consists of Charles "Pete" Conrad, Alan L. Bean, and Richard F. Gordon.

1970 — Southern Airways Flight 932 crashes in West Virginia, killing 75 including 37 members of the **Marshall University football team,** an event chronicled in the 2006 film *We Are Marshall.*

1971 — The unmanned NASA space probe Mariner 9 reaches Mars, becoming the **first spacecraft to orbit another planet.**

1973 — The **royal wedding** of Princess Anne and Captain Mark Phillips takes place in Westminster Abbey.

Apollo 12 Lunar Module pilot Alan L. Bean steps off the ladder onto the surface of the Moon.

Quote of the Day

"The ambition of the greatest men of our generation has been to wipe every tear from every eye. That may be beyond us, but so long as there are tears and suffering, so long our work will not be over."

Jawaharlal Nehru, first Prime Minister of India
born November 14, 1889

Births
and
Deaths
November 14

Charles, Prince of Wales (Photo: Arnaud Bouissou), born
November 14, 1948

Notable November 14 People

With the current world population at about seven billion people, on average about 19 million people also celebrate their birthdays on November 14 — and that isn't counting millions and millions who came before! No matter when you were born, you share your birthday with many special people whose accomplishments (and occasionally embarrassments) have been noted as part of history.

In this section, you'll meet fascinating people who share your birthday, or who died on this day in history. They're organized by what they're famous for, and then in reverse chronological order from most recent to earliest. Those who are shown in photographs or artwork have a box around them. We don't have photos of everyone, so please forgive us if your favorite person is missing.

Some of these people you've heard of, others will be new to you, but they all make up an important part of the reason that November 14 is a truly special day!

 Michael Dobson

Rocks at Belle-Ile, Port-Domois, by Claude Monet (1886)

Who Was Born on November 14?

Art and Illustration

John Steuart Curry, painter known for his work in the American Regionalism style. *(1897)*

Claude Monet, painter who helped found the French Impressionist school, known particularly for his paintings of lily ponds on his estate at Giverny. *(1840) (See also page 61.)*

Business and Society

Barbara Hutton, heiress of the Woolworth retail fortune, known as the "Poor Little Rich Girl" for her troubled personal life. *(1912)*

Government and Law

Condoleezza Rice, first African-American female Secretary of State, served in the administration of President George W. Bush. *(1954)*

Charles, Prince of Wales, eldest son of Queen Elizabeth II and longest-serving heir apparent to the British throne. *(1948) (Photo page 16)*

Hussein bin Talal of Jordan (حسين بن طلال), king of Jordan from 1952 until his death in 1999; widely recognized as a peacemaker in the Middle East. *(1935)*

Boutros Boutros-Ghali (بطرس بطرس غالي), Egyptian politician and diplomat who was the sixth Secretary-General of the United Nations. *(1922)*

Joseph McCarthy, Wisconsin senator known for his claims of Communist infiltration and for his smear tactics against accused Communists (which became known as "McCarthyism"); later censured by the Senate. *(1908)*

Jawaharlal Nehru, leader of the Indian independence movement who served as first Prime Minister of India. *(1889)*

William III of Orange, Dutch Prince of Orange who became King of England, Ireland, and Scotland in the "Glorious Revolution" of 1688. He ruled as joint sovereign with his wife Mary, daughter of deposed monarch King James VII and II, known as the reign of "William and Mary." *(1650)*

Literature and Journalism

Michael Dobbs, British politican and author best known for his *House of Cards* trilogy, adapted into both UK and a US television miniseries. *(1948)*

P. J. O'Rourke, conservative political satirist and journalist best known for his 1988 book *Holidays in Hell. (1947)*

Jawaharlal Nehru (left) with Mohandas K. Gandhi in 1946. (Photo: Dave Davis and Max Desfor)

Astrid Lindgren, Swedish writer best known as the creator of *Pippi Longstocking. (1907)*

Military and Space

Fred Haise, astronaut who flew on the ill-fated Apollo 13 mission. *(1933)*

Edward H. White II, astronaut on the Gemini 4 mission, first American to walk in space; died in the 1967 launch pad fire of Apollo 1. *(1930)*

Music

Yanni, Greek keyboardist and composer.known for his New Age compositions, and for his 1994 album and video *Live at the Acropolis. (1954)*

Stephen Bishop, singer-songwriter and actor whose hits include "On and On," "It Might Be You," and "Save It For a Rainy Day." *(1951)*

James Young, lead guitarist in the rock band Styx. *(1949)*

Buckwheat Zydeco, accordianist who became one of the first zydeco musicians to achieve mainstream success.*(1947)*

Wendy Carlos, electronic music composer known for her 1968 album (as Walter Carlos) *Switched-On Bach;* scored the films *A Clockwork Orange, The Shining,* and *Tron. (1939)*

The crew of Apollo 13: From left, James Lovell, John Swigert, and **Fred Haise**

Martha Tilton

Freddie Garrity, lead singer of the 1960s band Freddie and the Dreamers, whose best known hit was "I'm Telling You Now." *(1936)*

Martha Tilton, swing era singer best known for her 1939 hit "And the Angels Sing," with the Benny Goodman Orchestra. *(1915)*

Aaron Copeland, American composer whose best known works include *Appalachian Spring, Billy the Kid,* and *Fanfare for the Common Man. (1900)*

Fanny Mendelssohn, pianist and composer, sister of Felix Mendelssohn. *(1805)*

Leopold Mozart, conductor and composer best known as the father and teacher of Wolfgang Amadeus Mozart. *(1719)*

Performing Arts

Josh Duhamel, actor known for his roles in the *Transformers* film franchise, the soap opera *All My Children,* and *Las Vegas. (1972)*

Letitia Dean, English actress and singer best known as Sharon Watts on the BBC soap opera *EastEnders. (1967)*

Patrick Warburton, actor known for roles on *Seinfeld, The Tick, Rules of Engagement,* and *A Series of Unfortunate Events,* as well as for voice work on *Family Guy, The Emperor's New Groove,* and *The Venture Brothers. (1964)*

Laura San Giacomo, actress known for film roles in *Pretty Woman* and *Sex, Lies, and Video Tape,* and for the sitcom *Just Shoot Me! (1962)*

Paul McGann, actor best known as the 8th Doctor on the long-running science fiction series *Doctor Who. (1959)*

Paul Attanasio, screenwriter and producer who was nominated for the Academy Award for his screenplays for the films *Quiz Show* and *Donnie Brasco;* executive producer for the long-running TV series *House. (1959)*

Maggie Roswell, actress best known for her voice work on the animated series *The Simpsons,* and for film roles in *Lost in America* and *Pretty in Pink. (1952)*

McLean Stevenson, actor best known for playing Lt. Col. Henry Blake on the sitcom *M*A*S*H. (1927)*

Veronica Lake, actress known primarily for *femme fatale* roles. Her best known film is the 1941 comedy *Sullivan's Travels. (1922)*

Brian Keith, actor known for films including *The Parent Trap* and *The Wind and the Lion,* and for the television series *Family Affair. (1921)*

Sherwood Schwartz, television producer best known for the hits *Gilligan's Island* and *The Brady Bunch. (1916)*

Veronica Lake

Brian Keith

Louise Brooks, actress and dancer known as an icon of the "flapper," and popularizer of the bobbed haircut. *(1906)*

Louise Brooks (Photo: George Grantham Bain)

Dick Powell, actor who began his career in musical comedy before becoming known as a dramatic "tough guy." His best known films include *Double Indemnity* and *Murder, My Sweet;* hosted the early 1960s television anthology series *The Dick Powell Show. (1904)*

Science, Medicine, and Technology

Peter Norton, programmer best known for his Norton Utilities software suite. *(1943)*

Walter Jackson Freeman II, controversial American physician who specialized in lobotomy; traveled around the US in his "lobotomobile" performing lobotomies at various mental institutions, including the lobotomy of President John F.Kennedy's sister Rosemary. He did not have a medical degree, and was eventually banned from performing surgery after the death of nearly 100 patients. *(1895)*

Sir Frederick Banting, Canadian scientist who shared the 1923 Nobel Prize in Medicine or Physiology as co-discoverer of insulin. *(1891)*

Leo Baekland, chemist known as the "father of the plastics industry" for his invention of Bakelite. *(1863)*

Robert Fulton, engineer and inventor known for designing the first working submarine (the *Nautilus*) and for the first commercial steamboat, the *Clermont,* which carried passengers between New York City and Albany. *(1765)*

Robert Fulton's steamship *Clermont*

Sports

Curt Schilling, Major League Baseball pitcher, color analyst, and video game developer. *(1966)*

Willie Hernández, baseball pitcher for the Cubs, Phillies, and Tigers; third player to win the Cy Young Award, the MVP Award, and the World Series title in the same season. *(1954)*

Mike Katz, body builder and member of the New York Jets; known for his appearance with Arnold Schwartzenegger in the 1977 documentary *Pumping Iron. (1944)*

Dave Mackay, Scottish footballer (soccer player) named to both the English and Scottish Football Halls of Fame. *(1934)*

Jimmy Piersall, center fielder for 17 seasons in Major League Baseball; known for his battle with bipolar disorder chronicled in the book and film *Fear Strikes Out. (1929)*

Mabel Fairbanks, African-American figure skater and coach denied the right to compete in the Olympics qualifying event in her field; later toured internationally with the Ice Capades, and coached numerous figure skating starts including Kristi Yamaguchi and Tai Babilonia. Inducted into the US Figure Skating Hall of Fame as its first African-American member, and into the International Women's Sports Hall of Fame. *(1915)*

Sir Norman Brookes, Australian tennis player ranked World No. 1 in 1907; namesake of the Australian Open men's singles trophy, the Norman Brookes Challenge Cup and member of the International Tennis Hall of Fame. *(1877)*

Booker T. Washington (Photo: Harris & Ewing)

Who Died on November 14?

Part of the last generation of African-American leaders originally born into slavery, Booker T. Washington became the dominant leader in the civil rights struggle from the later years of the 19th century until his death..

Washington worked his way through college and graduate school, and was named the first leader of the Tuskegee Institute in Alabama, a new college founded for the higher education of black Americans, a post he would occupy for more than 30 years until his death.

In the post-Reconstruction South, widespread disenfranchisement and "Jim Crow" discriminatory laws hampered black advancement, and widespread lynchings of blacks suspected of challenging white dominance were taking place.

In his 1895 Atlanta address, Washington proposed a compromise in which blacks would not challenge segregation directly, but would instead focus the movement on education and entrepreneurship, especially in the form of African-American businesses. In exchange, he hoped to gain white support for these more modest goals, and to avoid the potential for a massive white backlash.

In spite of his public goals, he secretly funded court challenges to segregation and voting restrictions, funneling money to the NAACP and other organizations.

While most black leaders initially supported his "Atlanta compromise," this position became increasingly controversial. W. E. B. Du Bois and others established the NAACP to push for political change, but Washington's dominant leadership position and skills in media management and fund-raising made his strategy the dominant approach for a generation.

Washington was an accomplished orator and writer. He was the first African-American invited to the White House, the first to be featured on a US coin, and the first for whom a US Navy ship was named.

Booker T. Washington delivering his 1895 Atlanta Address

Other November 14 Deaths

Achievement

Grace Jones, British supercentenarian who was the world's seventh oldest person at the time of her death at the age of 113 years, 342 days; last known person in the British isles to have been born before the beginning of the 20th century. *(2013)*

Government and Politics

Policarpa Salavarrieta, seamstress and spy for the Revolutionary Forces during the Spanish Reconquista. Known as "La Pola," she is remembered as a heroine of the nation of Colombia; the date of her execution by Spanish forces is known as the Day of the Colombian Woman. *(1817) (Photo and more information on pages 44 and 45.)*

Nell Gwyn, actress best known as the long-time mistress of King Charles II of England and Scotland, also known for her comic wit. *(1687) (Photo page 36.)*

Alexander Nevsky (Алекса́ндр Не́вский), medieval Russian ruler who was Prince of Novgorod, Grand Prince of Kiev, and Grand Prince of Vladimir, known for his military victories. Canonized as a saint of the Russian Orthodox Church in 1547. *(1263)*

 Michael Dobson

Nell Gwyn, by Simon Pietersz Verelst

Justinian I, emperor of the Eastern Roman (Byzantine) Empire from 527 until his death in 565, called "the last Roman" for his attempts to reconquer the lost western half of the empire, at which he was partially successful. He oversaw a major rewriting of the Roman legal code, still used as the basis of civil law in many modern nations, and built the church of Hagia Sophia in Constantinople. He is known as a "nursing father" of the Christian church for his suppression of hereticism and his establishment of doctrine, for which he and his wife Theodora were canonized. *(565) (See also pages 48 and 49.)*

Literature and Journalism

Bob Trout, World War II8-era broadcast news reporter known as the "Iron Man of Radio" for his ability to handle difficult situations on the air; became one of the first broadcast anchormen, inspiring the long-running weekday radio news program *CBS World News Roundup* and television's *CBS Evening News.* (2000)

Jack Finney, science fiction writer best known for his books *The Body Snatchers* (basis for the 1956 film *Invasion of the Body Snatchers*), and the time travel romance *Time and Again.* (1995)

Saki (H. H. Munro), popular British writer known for his satires of Edwardian society and culture. (1916)

Performing Arts

Glen A. Larson, television producer who created *Battlestar Galactica, The Fall Guy, Magnum P.I., Knight Rider,* and other shows. *(2014)*

Gene Anthony Ray, actor who played dancer Leroy Johnson in the 1980 film *Fame* and its follow-on TV series. *(2003)*

Eddie Bracken, comic actor known for the 1944 films *Hail the Conquering Hero* and *The Miracle of Morgan Creek;* later films include *National Lampoon's Vacation* and *Rookie of the Year. (2002)*

Tony Richardson, English director and filmmaker who won the 1964 Academy Award for Best Director for the film *Tom Jones. (1991)*

Johnny Mack Brown (right) and Lois January in *Rogue of the Range* (1936, Supreme Pictures Corporation)

Johnny Mack Brown, College Football Hall of Fame player for the University of Alabama who went on to a film career; appeared in over 160 films. *(1974)*

Philosophy and Religion

A. C. Bhaktivedanta Swami Prabhupada (अभय चरणारवन्दि भक्तविदान्त स्वामी प्रभुपाद), founded the International Society for Krishna Consciousness, commonly known as the "Hare Krishna Movement." *(1977)*

Georg Wilhelm Friedrich Hegel, influential German philosopher. It was said, "All the great philosophical ideas of the past century—the philosophies of Marx and Nietzsche, phenomenology, German existentialism, and psychoanalysis—had their beginnings in Hegel." *(1831) (Photo page 40.)*

Science

Gottfried Leibniz, mathematician and philosopher who developed differential and integral calculus independently of Isaac Newton; also invented the Leibniz wheel, which was used in the "arithmometer," the first mass-produced mechanical calculator. *(1716) (Photo page 41.)*

Sports

Nick Bockwinkel, professional wrestler and actor inducted into the WWE Hall of Fame. *(2015)*

Georg Wilhelm Friedrich Hegel, by Jakob Schlesinger

Gottfired Wilhelm Leibniz, by Johann Friedrich Wentzel

Quote of the Day

"Success is to be measured not so much by the position that one has reached in life as by the obstacles which he has overcome while trying to succeed."

Booker T. Washington, political leader and educator, president of Tuskegee University died November 14, 1915

Holidays
Around
the World
November 14

Policarpa Salavarrieta, by José María Espionosa Prieto

Holidays Around the World

If you're looking for a reason to take your special day off, you should know that every single day is a holiday somewhere in the world! Here's some of what you can celebrate on November 14!

November 14 General Events

Anniversary of the Movement of Readjustment (Guinea-Bissau)

The West African nation of Guinea-Bissau celebrates a public holiday on November 14, commemorating the 1980 success of the revolutionary movement known as the African Party for the Independence of Guinea and Cape Verde (PAIGC).

Bal Diwas (India)

India celebrates Children's Day (Bal Diwas) on the November 14 birthday of independence leader and first Prime Minister Jawaharlal Nehru.

Day of the Colombian Woman (Colombia)

The South American nation of Colombia celebrates the women of its nation on the anniversary of the death of national heroine Policarpa Salavarrieta, a seamstress who spied for the revolutionary forces against Spanish Royalists. She was executed by the Spanish on November 14, 1817.

International Girls Day (worldwide)

The Confidence Coalition promotes International Girls Day each year on November 14, with the slogan "She Can Do Anything."

Hari Brigade Mobil (Indonesia)

Indonesia honors the formation of its special police operations force, known as Korps Brigade Mobil (BRIMOB), which took place November 14, 1946.

World Diabetes Day (international)

The International Diabetes Foundation leads a global awareness campaign for the disease each November 14. It marks the 1891 birthday of Frederick Banting, one of the pioneers in the discovery of insulin.

November 14 Food Holidays

National Guacamole Day (US)

In the United States, almost every day of the year is dedicated to a particular food. (Some other countries do this also, but not every day.) Sponsored by manufacturers, retailers, farmers, or simply fans, these days are often proclaimed by the President, Congress, state governors, or mayors. Given that there are more different foods than days of the year, some days honor more than one kind of food!

November 14 is **National Guacamole Day**. This tasty treat is made from avocados, sea salt, and lime juice, with some people adding tomato, onion, garlic, chili, cilantro, and jalapeño peppers.

Avocados are native to Central and South America, where they have been cultivated for more than ten thousand years. The Aztec name for avocado was *ahuacatl,* a word the Spanish explorers found difficult to pronouce, so they called it *aguacate* instead, from which we get the name "guacamole."

If guacamole isn't your thing, some people also observe November 14 as **National Pickle Day**. If November 14 falls on the second Sunday of the month, in El Salvador it's the **National Day of the Pupusa**, honoring one of its native dishes.

Guacamole (Photo: Nikodem Nijaki, CC BY-SA 3.0)

Honorary Food Months

In addition, the entire month of November is used to celebrate numerous foods. Here's a list of what to eat in the month of November!

- National Georgia Pecan Month
- National Peanut Butter Lover's Month
- National Pepper Month
- National Pomegranate Month
- National Raisin Bread Month

- Sweet Potato Awareness Month
- Vegan Month
- National Fun With Fondue Month

Cheese Fondue (for NATIONAL FUN WITH FONDUE MONTH).
(CC BY-SA 2.0)

Religious Feast Days and Holidays

Saint Days

Each day in the year is considered a feast day for one or more saints. In Western Christianity, November 14 is the feast day of Saints Joseph Pignatelli SJ, Emperor Justinian I (Lutheran Church), Laurence O'Toole, Nikola Tavelic, Samuel Seabury (Anglican Communion), and Serapion of Algiers.

In Eastern (Orthodox) Christianity, it is also the feast of Barlaam of Kiev, Justinian and Théodora,

Philip the Apostle, Stachys, Thomas II of
Constantinople, Veneranda, Dubricius, Sidonius of
Saint-Saëns, Malo of Brittany, Alberic of Utrecht,
Modanic, Eupemianos, Gregory Palmas, and Philip
of Novogorod. (These saints are commemorated on
November 1 by "Old Calendrists.*)

Sarah Bernhardt as Saint Théodora in the 1882 film *Théodora*,
directed by Victorien Sardou. (Photo: Félix Nadar)

---

* Old Calendrists use the Julian calendar, rather than the more
modern Gregorian calendar, for liturgical purposes. "New Style"
November 14 is the Gregorian equivalent of "Old Style" November
1. For more on different calendar types, see "What Day of the Week
is November 14?"

Moveable and Multi-Day Events

Some events take place over a specific week or time period. Start and finish dates may vary from year to year. Some events occur on different days each year (such as "fourth Saturday of a month"). These events sometimes include or take place on November 14.

Week-Long Celebrations

- Customer Service Week (US and Kenya)
- Geography Awareness Week
- National Nurse Practitioners Week
- National Split Pea Soup Week
- Mental Illness Awareness Week (US)
- World Kindness Week (week including November 13)

Moveable events that sometimes fall on November 14 include:

- Domino Day (2nd Friday)
- Father's Day (2nd Sunday in Estonia, Finland, Iceland, Norway, and Sweden)
- Grandparents Day, 2nd Sunday in South Sudan)
- International Day of Prayer for the Persecuted Church (2nd Sunday)
- National Tree Planting Day (2nd Saturday, Luxembourg)
- National Young Readers Day (2nd Tuesday)
- World Orphans Day (2nd Monday)

Dominoes, for DOMINO DAY (Photo: Gaz, CC BY-SA 3.0)

November Honorary Months

Presidents, Congresses, and nations around the world issue proclamations recognizing particular months to honor certain causes. These events generally fall in October, though honorary months do come and go. Holidays established by states and nonprofit organizations are listed if verified.

If not otherwise specified, all months are US. There is some variation from year to year; some celebratory months get added and others get dropped. Two places to get up to date information are the current edition of *Chase's Calendar of Events* or the website Brownielocks. Here are some honorary designations for November.

- Adopt a Turkey Month *(photo next page)*
- Aviation History Month

- Epilepsy Awareness Month
- Historic Bridge Awareness Month
- Military Family Appreciation Month
- National Adoption Month
- National Diabetes Month
- National Family Literacy Month
- National Hospice Month
- National Memoir Writing Month
- National Novel Writing Month (NaNoWriMo)
- World Sponge Month

Deček's Puranom, by Almanach (National Gallery of Slovenia — for
ADOPT A TURKEY MONTH

Just For Fun

Anybody can make up a holiday, and many people do! While most of these are not officially recognized, and some may come and go, here are a few more reasons to celebrate on November 14.

- International Selfie Day
- Loosen Up, Lighten Up Day
- National American Teddy Bear Day

The teddy bear is named for US President Theodore Roosevelt, based on an incident that took place in a bear hunt in Mississipi. This 1902 cartoon by Clifford Berryman was the first use of the name "teddy bear," and gave rise to the popular stuffed bear of the same name — for NATIONAL AMERICAN TEDDY BEAR DAY.

Quote of the Day

"November's night is dark and drear,
The dullest month of all the year."

Letitia Elizabeth Landon,
in *Traits and Trials of Early Life* (1836)

About
the
Month
of

November

November, by Joachim von Sandrart

November: The Eleventh Month

When shrieked
The bleak November winds, and smote the woods,
And the brown fields were herbless, and the shades
That met above the merry rivulet
Were spoiled, I sought, I loved them still; they seemed
Like old companions in adversity.

William Cullen Bryant, A Winter Piece

In Latin, *novem* means "nine," so it may seem strange that November is the eleventh month of the year. The original Roman calendar started in March, making November indeed the ninth month. No one is completely sure when the start of the year was moved to January, but the traditional name of November stuck.

In the northern hemisphere, November is a month in late autumn. In the southern hemisphere, November is in the springtime. May is its opposite month; spring in the north and fall in the south.

If it's not a Leap Year, November always starts on the same day of the week as February. If it is a leap year, November starts on the same day of the week as March.

November in Other Cultures

The month of November has different names in different languages. Some nations use calendars other than the Gregorian, and their months may overlap with November. In lunar-based calendars, such as the Islamic calendar, months move through the seasons. Still, many languages often have a word for November itself.

Arabic: نوفمبر (Nūfambar)

Chinese and Japanese: 十一月

Croatian: Studeni

Czech and Polish: Listopad

Finnish: Marraskuu

Greek: Νοέμβριος

Hebrew: נובמבר

Hindi: नवंबर

Old English: Blōtmōnaþ

Russian: ноябрь

November Sayings and Superstitions

Here are some sayings and superstitions associated with the month of November

- "A November bride will be liberal and kind, but sometimes cold."

- "Married in veils of November mist/Fortune your wedding ring has kissed."

- "If you wed in bleak November, only joys will come, remember."

November, by Eugène Grasset

November Symbols

Birthstone: Topaz (primarily yellow), and citrine. Topaz is associated with strength, tenacity, dedication and resilience. Citrine is supposed to encourage vitality and promote good health.

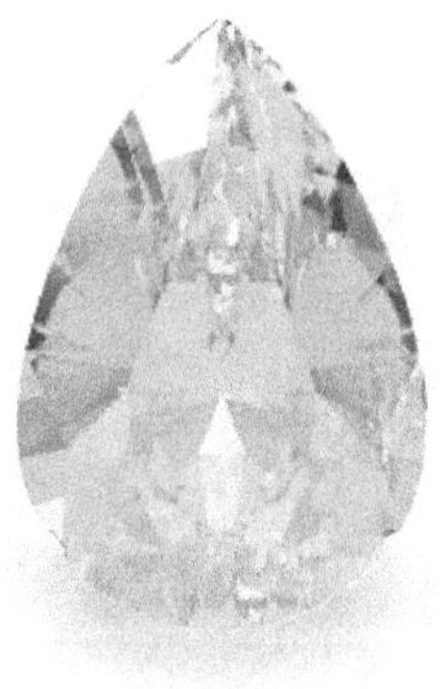

Citrine

Birth Flower: Chrysanthemum. The Chrysanthemum is associated with compassion, friendship,and joy. Red is for love, white for innocence, and yellow for unrequited love.

Chrysanthemums, by Claude Monet

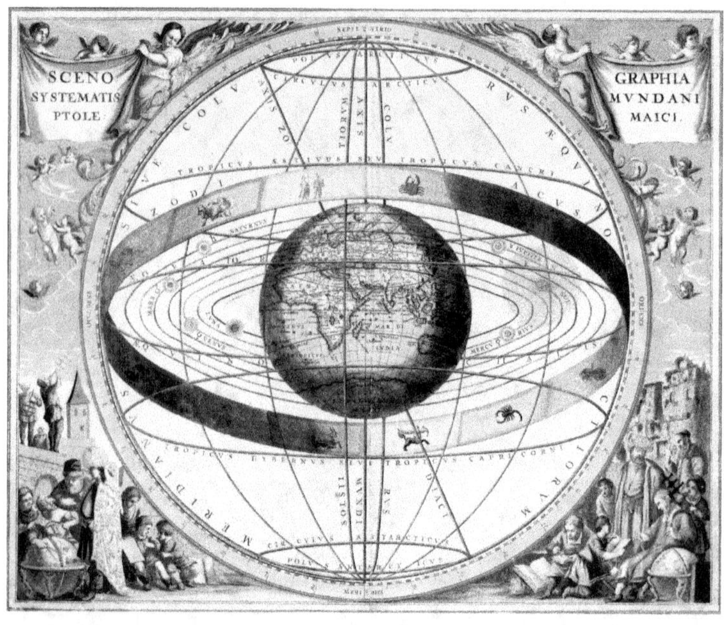

Scenography of the Ptolemaic Cosmography, by Johannes van Loon, based on Andreas Cellarius's *Harmonia Macrocosmica,* 1660

November 14 Zodiac Signs

From the perspective of someone on Earth, the Sun appears to move through the sky throughout the year, along a path astronomers call the *ecliptic plane*. The ecliptic plane is divided into twelve constellations, known as the zodiac, based on traditionally observed patterns of stars. On your birthday, you can't see your constellation, because it's in the daytime sky.

The zodiac was first developed by Babylonian astronomers about 2,500 years ago. Because they were unaware that the Earth wobbles like a spinning top (known as *precession*), they didn't make allowance for the fact that the Sun's path through the zodiac changes over time.

That means there are now two sets of dates for your birth sign. The *tropical dates* are the original Babylonian dates; the *sidereal dates* tell you where the Sun actually appears as it moves along its annual path.

For November 14, the tropical sign is **Scorpio** and the sidereal sign is **Libra**.

Libra

Tropical September 23 to October 23
Sidereal October 16 to November 15

The Babylonians considered Libra, the Scales, to be sacred to the sun god Shamash, patron of truth and justice. The Romans reassigned the scales to Astraea, the celestial virgin, better known as Virgo.

Libra is an air sign, and people born under this sign are supposed to be extroverts, socially graceful, and just. Librans are supposed to be compatible with the other air signs of Gemini and Aquarius.

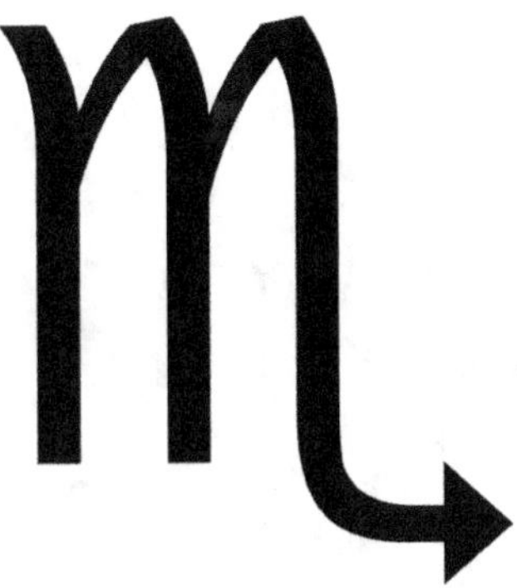

Scorpio

Tropical October 23 to November 21
Sidereal November 16 to December 15

Scorpio, the Scorpion, appears in the Greek myth of the hunter Orion. Because Orion had touched the robes of the goddess Artemis, in revenge, the goddess had the scorpion kill Orion. As a reward, she placed the scorpion in the sky, where it chases Orion through the eternal night.

Scorpio is a fire sign, and people born under this sign are supposed to be determined, reserved, loyal, and secretive. Scorpios are supposed to be compatible with the water signs of Pisces and Capricorn.

Illustration by Edward Penfield

What Day of the Week is November 14?

On what day of the week does November 14 fall?

Surprisingly, this isn't an easy question. Because the calendar year is 365 days long (366 in leap years), it doesn't divide evenly by the seven days of the week.

Also, the Earth goes around the Sun in about 365-1/4 days, so a calendar tends to drift over time. That's why the same date falls on different weekdays in different years.

This is made even more complicated by a change in calendars that took place in 1582. Our modern calendar has its roots in ancient Rome, in a calendar reform conducted by Julius Caesar. Caesar commissioned mathematicians to attack the problem, and they came up with the idea of leap years, and thus standardized the calendar for centuries to come. This was called the Julian calendar.

Over time, however, the small errors in Caesar's calculation compounded. That's why Pope Gregory XIII commissioned the Gregorian calendar, used in most of the world today. Some countries converted in 1582, when the calendar was first developed; some converted later; other still haven't changed.

Gregorian and Julian aren't the only types of calendars. The Hebrew year, the Islamic year, and many other calendars are used in different parts of the world and among different people.

You can convert Gregorian dates to other calendars, including the Hebrew calendar, the Islamic calendar, and even the Mayan calendar by visiting the Fourmilab Calendar Converter at http://www.fourmilab.ch/documents/calendar/.

Chinese calendar systems are quite complex and have changed several times; a full discussion is far beyond the scope of this book. If you're interested, you can find information here: http://www.hermetic.ch/cal_stud/chinese_cal.htm.

On Names and Dates

Historians use "CE" (Common Era) and "BCE" (Before the Common Era) instead of the more common "AD" (Anno Domini, or Year of Our Lord) and "BC" (Before Christ), reflecting the fact that the year-numbering system established by the Gregorian calendar is used throughout the world in many countries not culturally Christian.

The CE/BCE designation dates back to at least 1708, and has been adopted as a standard by the United Nations and the Universal Postal Union. Because this series of books covers events and people of all nations and cultures, we use the CE/BCE terms.

The abbreviation "O.S." ("Old Style") on some dates refers to the fact that the Russian Empire did not switch from the Julian to the Gregorian calendar at the same time as the rest of Europe, and therefore some figures and events have two dates.

Also, in the Julian calendar in England in the 16th century, the year began on March 25 rather than January 1. To avoid confusion with Gregorian dates, dates between January and March were often written using both years.

People and events whose original names are not in the Western alphabet have their native names (where possible) in the appropriate script shown in parenthesis. If you are using an e-reader to access an electronic version of this book, all characters don't always display on all devices.

A 50-year brass perpetual calendar.

Quote of the Day

"Time is an illusion, lunchtime doubly so."

Douglas Adams,
from *The Hitchhiker's Guide to the Galaxy*

Notes and Credits
Timespinner Press

Cartoon by John T. McCutcheon

Copyright, Credit, and Contact

Follow Us

Our blog "This Day in History" (http://timespinnerpress.com/this-day-in-history/) features short articles on events and people associated with each day, and updates several times each week. Also subscribe to the "Quote of the Day" at http://timespinnerpress.com/quote-of-the-day/. You can get daily links by following us on Facebook at TimespinnerPress, or on Twitter as @sidewisethinker.

Contact Us

Find an error or a format problem? Want information about the series, about us, or about when the volume for your special day might be available? Please email us at editor@timespinnerpress.com. (We also take requests if your special day isn't yet complete. Please give us at least six weeks' notice if possible.)

Sources

We owe a great debt to Wikipedia, which is our first stop for research. We attempt to make independent confirmation of all important dates and facts through a variety of other sources.

Other sources we frequently use include the Library of Congress; "on this day" listings from *Encyclopedia Britannica, the New York Times,* and the BBC; Omniglot for the names of months in other languages; *Chase's Calendar of Events;* and, of course, the always essential Google.

All art and photographs are either in the public domain, used under a Creative Commons license, or with a "fair use" justification, and most frequently come from Wikimedia Commons and the Library of Congress Prints and Photographs Division.

Attribution is provided where possible, or as requested by the copyright owner, or when there is particular historical significance, listed below. For information about any particular illustration or photograph, please contact us.

Credits

1. The November 14, 1910, cover photograph "First Airplane Takeoff from a Warship" is from the collection of the Naval History and Heritage Command, Photo #NH 77601. It is in the public domain as a work created by an employee of the US government as part of that person's official duties.

2. The illustration of the month of November used on the back cover is from the French Gothic illuminated manuscript *Les Très Riches Heures du duc de Berry* by the Limbourg Brothers, Jean Colombe, and an intermediate painter whose name is lost to history. It is in the public domain because its copyright has expired.

3. The box graphic used on the first page is from a 1916 pamphlet entitled "Divorce versus Democracy" authored by G. K. Chesterton, originally published in London by the Society of St. Peter and St. Paul. It is in the public domain in the US because it was published prior to 1923, and is in the public domain in all countries (including the country of origin) in which the copyright time is the author's life plus 70 years or less.

4. The graphic design for the section pages in this book is from a design originally created for a pharmacy label. It is courtesy of Wellcome Images (ICV No 11073, photo V0010813), and is used here under CC BY-SA 4.0.

5. The painting "November" from *Labors of the Month* by Simon Bening, was originally published in the first half of the 16th

century, and is in the public domain because its copyright has expired.

6. The 1911 photograph of Eugene Ely is from the collection of the US Naval History and Heritage Command, NH 77599. It is in the public domain because its copyright has expired.

7. The 1911 photograph of the first airplane landing on a warship is from the collection of the US Naval History and Heritage Command, NH 82737. It is in the public domain as a work created by an employee of the US government as part of that person's official duties.

8. The photograph of Nellie Bly by H. J. Myers was taken circa 1890 and is in the public domain because its copyright has expired. It is from the Library of Congress collection, digital ID cph.3b22819.

9. The 1941 photograph of Winston Churchill touring the ruins of Coventry Cathedral is from the collection of the Imperial War Museums, image H 14250. It is in the public domain as a work created by the UK government prior to June 1, 1957.

10. The painting "The Problem We All Live With" by Norman Rockwell remains under copyright until 2059. It is used here under "fair use" provisions of US copyright law. It is a historically significant image of a historically significant event. No free alternative exists. It is a low-resolution image not suitable for the creation of counterfeit merchandise or the creation of illegal copies and it does not limit the copyright owner's rights to sell the image in any way. The use of the image of six-year old Ruby Bridges in this context follows the same "fair use" rationale.

11. The US Army photograph of combat operations in the Battle of Ia Drang is in the public domain as a work created by an employee of the US government as part of that person's official duties.

12. The photograph of Apollo 11 astronaut Alan L. Bean exiting the lunar module is in the public domain as a work created solely by NASA.

13. The 2015 photograph of Charles, Prince of Wales, is by Arnaud Bouissou, who dedicated it to the public domain under CC0 1.0.

14. The 1886 painting *Rocks at Belle-Ile, Port-Domois* by Claude Monet is in the Cincinnati Art Museum, and the image used here is courtesy Google Art Project. It is in the public domain because its copyright has expired.

15. The 1945 photograph of Jawaharlal Nehru and Mohandas K. Gandhi was taken by Max Desfor and credited to Dave Davis. It is in the public domain in India, its country of origin, because its is more than 50 years old. It is in the public domain in the US because it was first published in the US between 1923 and 1977 without a copyright notice.

16. The 1970 photograph of the Apollo 13 crew is in the public domain as a work solely created by NASA.

17. The photograph of Martha Tilton appeared on the cover of the April 1946 issue of *Radio Mirror.* It is in the public domain because it was published in the US between 1923 and 1953, and although there was a copyright notice, the copyright was not renewed.

18. The 1952 publicity photograph of Veronica Lake is in the public domain because it was first published in the US between 1923 and 1977 without a copyright notice. Traditionally, publicity photographs are not copyrighted because of the way they are intended to be used.

19. The 1957 publicity photograph of Brian Keith is in the public domain because it was first published in the US between 1923 and 1977 without a copyright notice.

20. The 1927 photograph of Louise Brooks by George Grantham Bain is in the public domain according the the Library of Congress. It is from the George Grantham Bain collection at the Library, with digital ID ggbain.32453.

21. The illustration of the steamship *Clermont* is in the public domain because its copyright has expired. It is courtesy Project Gutenberg.

22. The 1905 portrait of Booker T. Washington was taken by Harris & Ewing, and is part of the Harris & Ewing collection at the Library of Congress (digital ID ppmsca.23961). It is in the public domain because its copyright has expired. The image has been cropped.

23. The 1895 photograph of Booker T. Washington giving his Atlanta Address is in the public domain because its copyright has expired.

24. The portrait of Nell Gwyn by Simon Pietersz Verelst was painted circa 1680, and is in the public domain because its copyright has expired. The painting is in the National Portrait Gallery, London.

25. The screenshot from the 1936 film *Rogue of the Range* is in the public domain because the film was released in the US between 1923 and 1953, and although there was a copyright notice, the copyright was not renewed.

26. The 1831 painting of Hegel by Jakob Schlesinger is in the public domain because its copyright has expired. It is in the Alte Nationalgalerie, Berlin, Germany.

27. The painting of Gottfried Leibniz by Johann Friedrich Wentzel was created circa 1700, and is in the public domain because its copyright has expired.

28. The 1855 painting of Policarpa Salavarrieta ("La Pola") is by José María Espionosa Prieto is in the public domain in its home country of Colombia and in other nations that limit copyright to the life of the author plus 70 years.

29. The 2011 photograph of guacamole is by Nikodem Nijaki, and is used here under CC BY-SA 3.0.

30. The 2009 photograph of cheese fondue is by "The Junes" and modified by "Zitronenpresse."It is used here under CC BY-SA 2.0.

31. The 1882 photograph of Sarah Bernhardt by Felix Nadar is in the public domain because its copyright has expired.

32. The photograph of dominoes is by "Gaz," and is used here under CC BY-SA 3.0.

33. The 17th century painting *Deček's Puranom* by Almanach is from the collection of the National Gallery of Slovenia (NGS3100). It is in the public domain because its copyright has expired.

34. The "Teddy Bear" cartoon by Clifford Berryman originally appeared in the November 16, 1902, issue of the *Washington Post*. It is in the public domain because its copyright has expired.

35. The painting "November" by Joachim von Sandrart was created in 1643, and is in the public domain because its copyright has expired. The original can be seen in the Staatsgalerie im Neuen Schloss, Schleißheim, Austria.

36. The 1896 postcard "November" by Eugène Grasset is in the public domain because its copyright has expired.

37. The photograph of a citrine is by Les Facettes and is used here under CC BY-SA 3.0.

38. The 1882 painting of chrysanthemums by Claude Monet is in the public domain because its copyright has expired. The painting is in the collection of the Metropolitan Museum of Art, New York.

39. The celestial sphere is from *Scenography of the Ptolemaic Cosmography,* by Johannes van Loon, based on Andreas Cellarius's *Harmonia Macrocosmica,* 1660. It is in the public domain because its copyright has expired.

40. The 1906 automobile calendar is by Edward Penfield, and is in the collection of the Library of Congress Prints and Photographs Division. It is in the public domain because its copyright has expired.

41. The 50-year perpetual calendar photograph is in the public domain.

42. The cartoon by John T. McCutcheon is from his 1905 collection *The Mysterious Stranger and Other Cartoons by John T. McCutcheon.* It is in the public domain because its copyright has expired.

43. The 1879 painting "November" by John Grimshaw is in the public domain because its copyright has expired.

44. The painting "November" is from the *Brevarium Grimani,* circa 1510, and is in the public domain because its copyright has expired.

License Description and Terms

Aside from material purely in the public domain, photographs and other material in this book are used under specific licenses permitting free use, usually with an attribution requirement. For full text and terms of these licenses, click or enter the appropriate links below. If you believe there is an error in the copyright status or attribution of any of these images, please email us.

- Creative Commons Attribution 2.0 Generic (CC-BY 2.0): http://creativecommons.org/licenses/by/2.0/deed.en
- Creative Commons Attribution-Share Alike 3.0 Generic (CC-BY-SA 3.0): http://creativecommons.org/licenses/by-sa/3.0/
- Creative Commons Attribution-Share Alike 2.5 Generic (CC-BY-SA 2.5): http://creativecommons.org/licenses/by-sa/2.5/deed.en
- Creative Commons Attribution-Share Alike 2.0 Generic (CC-BY-SA 2.0): http://creativecommons.org/licenses/by/2.0/deed.en
- Creative Commons Attribution-Share Alike 1.0 Generic (CC-BY-SA 1.0): http://creativecommons.org/licenses/by-sa/1.0/deed.en
- CC0 1.0 Universal (CC0 1.0) Public Domain Dedication (CC0 1.0) http://creativecommons.org/publicdomain/zero/1.0/deed.en
- GNU Free Documentation License (GFDL): http://en.wikipedia.org/wiki/Wikipedia:Text_of_the_GNU_Free_Documentation_License
- License Art Libre (Free Art License): http://artlibre.org

November, by John Atkinson Grimshaw

Other Books from Timespinner Press

The Story of a Special Day

Michael Dobson

A series of (eventually) 366 volumes covering everything that happened on your special day! Events, births, deaths, quotes, holidays, and much more. It's like a birthday card they'll never throw away!

US$7.95 print / US$2.99 ebook.

From Plassey to Pakistan

Humayun Mirza

The history of British Colonial India and the formation of Pakistan from the unique perspective of the son of Pakistan's first president and last of the royal line of Bengal, Bihar, and Orissa! This unique historical document tells the inside story of this distinguished family, including the detailed story of the coup that toppled his father from power!

US$27.95 print

A Whole New Navy: America's War in the Pacific

Miles Durr

The most comprehensive and detailed description of America's naval war in the Pacific ever—every battle, every ship, every task force and every task group from Pearl Harbor through the Japanese surrender! A must-have for the collection of every World War II buff!

US$29.95 print

Improbable History: The Weird, the Obscure, and the Strangely Important

edited by Michael Dobson

From the birth of Western civilization to the rescue of Apollo 13, from the Leaning Tower of Pisa to Florence's Duomo, history has often turned on small, improbable details. Whatever happened to the ancient Samaritan people? Why did a fortuitous rainstorm allow the British to conquer India? How did an air raid in Italy lead to the development of chemotherapy? What happened when Albert Einstein met Adolf Hitler on the streets of Berlin? How did the Japanese manage to attack the US mainland using balloons? A cast of award-winning writers tackle some of the strangest tales in history!

US$19.95 print

The Letters of William Philip Schwartz 1842-1855

edited by John F. Schwartz

The 19th century soldier and adventurer William Philip Schwartz wrote a series of vivid and detailed letters chronicling his adventures in the Indian Wars, the Mexican-American War, the Gold Rush, and his term as Marine sergeant aboard the USS Constellation. A pioneer in photography, he took *the first known war photographs*. An unforgettable first-hand look into life in the 19th century!

US$17.95 print

Timespinner
Press

www.timespinnerpress.com

November, from the *Brevarium Grimani* (c.1510)